# Emergent Literacy Survey/K-2

## John J. Pikulski

## Overview

The Emergent Literacy Survey can be used to assess quickly and efficiently several areas that are highly related to success in beginning reading. It can be used by classroom teachers or reading specialists.

Administering the entire Survey to a child would take over thirty minutes. However, the Survey is meant to be used flexibly. Based on your experience with the Survey and with the children being tested, you can decide on a combination of tasks that are most useful to you. Later in this manual, suggestions are offered for reducing the administration time by using selected tasks from the Survey.

### Purposes of the Emergent Literacy Survey

- To obtain baseline data: The Survey can be used to document the emerging literacy skills that children bring with them to kindergarten, to first grade, or to an intervention or remediation program.

- To chart progress: The Survey can be re-administered to assess growth in those areas it measures.

- To identify areas of strength and needs: The Survey can aid in determining children's strengths to be developed and in uncovering areas where children show limited development and might profit from instruction that would build a foundation for reading and writing skills.

- To identify children needing early intervention: Along with teacher observations, the Survey can assist in identifying children who will need the support of an early intervention program.

- To evaluate program effectiveness: The Survey can be used to evaluate the effectiveness of kindergarten, early intervention, special education, and remedial reading programs.

## Areas Assessed

| | |
|---|---|
| **PHONEMIC AWARENESS** | • Rhyme<br>• Beginning Sounds<br>• Blending Onsets and Rimes<br>• Segmenting Onsets and Rimes<br>• Phoneme Blending<br>• Phoneme Segmentation |
| **FAMILIARITY WITH PRINT** | • Concepts of Print<br>• Letter Naming |
| **BEGINNING READING AND WRITING** | • Word Recognition<br>• Word Writing<br>• Sentence Dictation |

# General Guidelines for Administering the Survey

## Individual or Group Administration

The Survey is designed to be administered to one child at a time; the Word Writing and Sentence Dictation tasks, however, can be administered to small groups of children.

## Practice Items

Most sections of the Survey begin with three items that are not scored but are included as Practice Items in order to familiarize a child with the activity to be performed. All Practice Items should be used regardless of a child's success with them. If a child is successful, move through the items. If a child fails to respond or responds incorrectly, give the correct response or examples of responses as indicated in Directions.

Directions should be followed, as given, if the results of the Survey are to be shared with other teachers or professionals. Misinterpretations of the results can occur if a child is given an unusual amount of instruction and support— either more or less than indicated in Directions.

HOUGHTON MIFFLIN

# EMERGENT LITERACY SURVEY/K-2

## WITH PHONEMIC AWARENESS SCREENING

## INVITATIONS
### TO LITERACY

K
through
2

54248

## Acknowledgments

Special thanks to Barbara M. Taylor, University of Minnesota, and to the teachers and advisors of the University of Delaware Ready Success from the Start Project for their contributions to the development of the Emergent Literacy Survey.

# Assessment Items

After the three Practice Items have been completed, a child should not be told the correct responses to succeeding items. Praise and encouragement may be offered from time to time. ("Good job." "You really are working hard at this.") Avoid giving feedback as to whether responses are correct or not. If you indicate some responses are correct, many children will infer that all other responses are incorrect.

Blackline Masters in large print suitable for young readers are provided on pages 21–26 for use with sections assessing Concepts of Print, Letter Naming, and Word Recognition. Recording Forms are provided on pages 27–30.

# Recording and Scoring

All responses should be recorded immediately. For most areas a check mark (✓) can be used to indicate a correct response. Incorrect responses should be recorded since the nature of the error can sometimes be informative.

For most of the tasks on the Survey, the score is simply the number of correct items. More detailed scoring directions and scoring examples are given for the Word Writing and Sentence Dictation tasks.

# Discontinuing Testing

In order to avoid children's frustration or to save time, you may decide to discontinue testing. For tasks with eight items, omit the remaining items of a task if a child fails to respond to the Practice Items and the first three Assessment Items. For tasks that have other than eight items, use the suggestions for discontinuing tasks that are given under Discontinue.

# Selective Use of Tasks in Kindergarten

The Emergent Literacy Survey was designed primarily for use with kindergarten and first grade children, but it can be used with older children who are encountering substantial problems in learning to read.

The Survey can be administered at any time during the kindergarten year. Some teachers use it at the beginning of the year in order to obtain baseline data for children. (Which emerging literacy skills do these young children already possess? Which need to be developed?) Young children enter kindergarten with a wide range of emerging literacy skills. Beginning kindergarten children should not be expected to possess these skills, though some will. The areas measured by the Emergent Literacy Survey are ones that can be expected to be developed, given the appropriate instruction and opportunities, during the course of the kindergarten year. Thus, a comparison of beginning and end of kindergarten scores can serve as a measure of progress.

If you do not wish to use the entire Survey with kindergarten children, particularly at the beginning of the year, you may want to make the following adjustments.

## PHONEMIC AWARENESS

▶ Since Rhyme and Beginning Sounds tasks are among the most fundamental in the area of phonemic awareness, these sections should be administered to kindergarten children. However, in order to avoid frustration and to save time, testing may be discontinued if a child is not familiar with these concepts and misses three assessment items on either of these tasks.

Blending Onsets and Rimes and Segmenting Onsets and Rimes are more advanced phonemic awareness skills. These sections might be omitted completely if a child was unsuccessful with Rhyme or Beginning Sounds.

Blending Phonemes and Segmenting Phonemes are among the most advanced phonemic awareness skills, and these sections might be used only with children who were successful with the Onsets and Rimes tasks.

## FAMILIARITY WITH PRINT

▶ Concepts of Print are fundamental, and this section should be administered. If a kindergarten child has difficulty with the first three items, omit the tracking print and spoken/written word correspondence items.

Letter Naming is a fundamental task, and many teachers are interested in knowing whether their kindergarten children are familiar with letter names. If a child fails to recognize any of the first ten capital letters, the Letter Naming task may be discontinued. Young children who cannot name capital letters are seldom able to name lower case letters.

## BEGINNING READING AND WRITING

▶ Omit the Word Recognition Test for kindergarten children who identified fewer than ten letters on the Letter Naming task.

The Directions for Word Writing may be modified. Simply ask children if they can write their names. If they are successful in doing this, ask them if there are other words they can write, and proceed with the standard administration of the task.

The Sentence Dictation section may be omitted if children identify fewer than five words on the Word Recognition test; otherwise, proceed with the suggested administration and discontinuation directions.

# Selective Use of Tasks for First Grade or Older Children Receiving Special Instruction in Reading

### PHONEMIC AWARENESS

▶ To save time, begin with the Onsets and Rimes measures. If a child is successful, continue with the Phoneme tasks. Only if a child encounters difficulty with the Onsets and Rimes or the Phoneme measures is it necessary to administer the Rhyme and Beginning Sounds tasks.

### FAMILIARITY WITH PRINT

▶ Letter Naming could begin with the lower case letters. If virtually all lower case letters are identified, it can be assumed that all capital letters will be known, and this test may be bypassed.

The Word Recognition task could precede the Concepts of Print section. If a child identifies fifteen of the thirty words correctly on the Word Recognition test, the Concepts of Print test may be omitted.

### BEGINNING READING AND WRITING

▶ The Word Recognition Test, Word Writing, and Sentence Dictation are important measures and should not be omitted. Guidelines for discontinuing testing may be followed.

# Specific Directions for the Survey

## Phonemic Awareness

### RHYME

▶ **Directions**  When words rhyme, they sound the same at the end.  For example, *fun, run,* and *sun* rhyme.  I'm going to say a word, and I want you to give me a word that rhymes with my word.

▶ **Practice Items**  **Listen to this word – *dig.*  Tell me a word that rhymes with *dig.*** (If necessary, give examples: *big, pig, fig, wig* all rhyme with *dig.*)

*dark* **– Tell me a word that rhymes with *dark.***  (Examples: *bark, park.*)

*boy* **– Tell me a word that rhymes with *boy.***  (Examples: *joy, toy.*)

▶ **Assessment Items**  (Do not provide any help with these items or tell a child whether the response is correct.)

_____.  **Tell me a word that rhymes with** _____.

1. *bat*
2. *head*
3. *fan*
4. *got*

5. *rug*
6. *be*
7. *fog*
8. *mill*

▶ **Recording**  On Recording Form I, page 27, indicate correct responses with ✓. If a child gives an incorrect word, write that word.  Write **0** if the child does not respond.

▶ **Discontinue**  Discontinue testing if a child misses three consecutive items after the Practice Items.

### BEGINNING SOUNDS

▶ **Directions**  Words can begin with the same sound.  Listen to these words: *boy, ball,* and *balloon.*  All of these words begin with the same sound /b/* – *boy, ball, balloon,* /b/.

▶ **Practice Items**

*ride* **– Tell me a word that begins with the same sound as *ride,* /r/.**  (If necessary, give examples: *red, race, rhyme, run, Roger* all begin with /r/.)

**jam** – **Tell me a word that begins with the same sound as** *jam,* **/j/.** (Examples: *jet, jump, just, job, Jill* all begin with /j/.)

**girl** – **Tell me a word that begins with the same sound as** *girl,* **/g/.** (Examples: *give, get, go, game, Garfield* all begin with /g/.)

▶ **Assessment Items** (Do not provide any help with these items.)

_____ **Tell me a word that begins with the same sound as** _____ **/_ /.**

1. **sink** /s/
2. **pie** /p/
3. **more** /m/
4. **donkey** /d/

5 **lion** /l/
6. **fast** /f/
7. **children** /ch/
8. **balloon** /b/

▶ **Recording** On Recording Form I, page 27, indicate correct responses with ✓. If a child gives an incorrect word, write that word. If a child gives a sound, write the letter that sound represents between two slash marks, for example, /r/. Write **0** if a child does not respond.

▶ **Discontinue** Discontinue testing if a child misses three consecutive items after the Practice Items.

*Note: Whenever a letter appears between two slash marks, as /b/, the person giving this Survey should say the sound for this letter, not the name of the letter.*

*Note 2: Some children will continue to give rhyming words here as they did for the first task. Provide corrective feedback on the Practice Items. Explain that you asked for a word that begins with the same sound—not a rhyming word. Children who continue giving rhyming words have not developed a clear concept of beginning sounds. Some teachers feel that giving the Beginning Sounds task immediately after the Rhyme task creates an interference for some children. Sometimes teachers prefer to administer the Onsets and Rimes tasks or even a Familiarity with Print task, and then return to the Beginning Sounds task. This is permissible.*

## BLENDING ONSETS AND RIMES

▶ **Directions** Sometimes you can add a sound to the beginning of a word and make a new word. If I have the word *at,* and I add the /s/ sound at the beginning of *at,* I make the word *sat:* /s/*at, sat.*

▶ **Practice Items** **What word do I have if I add the /p/ sound at the beginning of** *ink***? /p/***ink***?** (Give the word *pink,* if needed.)

**What word do I have if I add the /m/ sound at the beginning of** *eat***? /m/***eat***?** (Give the word *meat,* if needed.)

**What word do I have if I add the /d/ sound at the beginning of** *ear***? /d/***ear***?** (Give the word *dear,* if needed.)

► **Assessment Items** (Provide no additional help with these items.)

**What word do I have if I add the /__ / sound at the beginning of _____?**
**/__/_____**

1. /m/*an*
2. /f/*all*
3. /t/*able*
4. /b/*ill*

5. /r/*at*
6. /g/*old*
7. /m/*other*
8. /l/*earn*

► **Recording** On Recording Form I, page 27, indicate correct responses with ✓. If a child gives an incorrect word, write that word. If a child gives a sound, write the letter that sound represents between two slash marks, for example, /r/. Write **0** if a child does not respond.

► **Discontinue** Discontinue testing if a child misses three consecutive items after the Practice Items.

## SEGMENTING ONSETS AND RIMES

► **Directions** Sometimes you can take a sound away from the beginning of a word and make a new word. If I had the word *bad* and took the /b/ sound away, I would have the new word *add.*

► **Practice Items** **What word would I have if I took the /b/ sound from the beginning of *bake*? /b/ from *bake*?** (ache)

**What word would I have if I took the /p/ sound from the beginning of *part*? /p/ from *part*?** (art)

**What word would I have if I took the /f/ sound from the beginning of *fox*? /f/ from *fox*?** (ox)

► **Assessment Items** (Provide no additional help with these items.)

**What word would I have if I took the /__ / sound from the beginning of _____?**
**/__ / from _____?**

1. /f/ *fit* (it)
2. /g/ *gate* (ate)
3. /s/ *sink* (ink)
4. /l/ *land* (and)

5. /b/ *bend* (end)
6. /p/ *pup* (up)
7. /sh/ *shape* (ape)
8. /k/ *couch* (ouch)

► **Recording** On Recording Form I, page 27, indicate correct responses with ✓. If a child gives an incorrect word, write that word. If a child gives a sound, write the letter that sound represents between two slash marks, for example, /r/. Write **0** if a child does not respond.

► **Discontinue** Discontinue testing if a child misses three consecutive items after the Practice Items.

## PHONEME BLENDING

► **Directions** Words are made by putting sounds together. I am going to say the sounds, and I want you to tell me what word they make. For example, /s/ /a/ /t/ make the word *sat.*

► **Practice** Items

**/b/ /ĕ/ /d/ What word would I have if I put together the sounds /b/ /ĕ/ /d/?** (If needed, say /b/ /ĕ/ /d/ makes *bed.*)

**/m/ /ă/ /p/ What word would I have if I put together the sounds /m/ /ă/ /p/?** (If needed, say /m/ /ă/ /p/ makes *map.*)

**/l/ /ŏ/ /s/ /t/ What word would I have if I put together the sounds /l/ /ŏ/ /s/ /t/?** (If needed, say /l/ /ŏ/ /s/ /t/ makes *lost.*)

► **Assessment Items** (Provide no additional help with these items.)

**/_/ /_/ /_/ What word would I have if I put together the sounds /_/ /_/ /_/?**

| | |
|---|---|
| 1. **/t/ /ă/ /p/** *(tap)* | 5. **/l/ /ĭ/ /d/** *(lid)* |
| 2. **/m/ /ĕ/ /n/** *(men)* | 6. **/b/ /ī/ /k/** *(bike)* |
| 3. **/j/ /ŏ/ /g/** *(jog)* | 7. **/w/ /ā/ /v/** *(wave)* |
| 4. **/k/ /ŭ/ /t/** *(cut)* | 8. **/s/ /ŏ/ /f/ /t/** *(soft)* |

► **Recording** On Recording Form 2, page 28, indicate correct responses with ✓. If a child gives an incorrect word, write that word. If a child gives a sound, write the letter that sound represents between two slash marks, e.g., /r/. Write **0** if a child does not respond.

► **Discontinue** Discontinue testing if a child misses three consecutive items after the Practice Items.

## PHONEME SEGMENTATION

► **Directions** Now I will say a word and I want you to tell me the sounds that are in the word. For example, if I said *sat,* you would say /s/ /ă/ /t/.

► **Practice Items What are the sounds in *mud*? Think about the first sound, the next sound, and the last sound.** (If necessary say, the sounds in *mud* are /m/ /ŭ/ /d/.)

**What are the sounds in *not*? Think about the first sound, the next sound, and the last sound.** (If necessary say, the sounds in *not* are /n/ /ŏ/ /t/.)

**What are the sounds in *jump*? Think about the first sound, the next sound, and the last sound.** (If necessary say, the sounds in *jump* are /j/ /ŭ/ /m/ /p/.)

▶ Assessment Items (Provide no additional help with these items.)

**What are the sounds in _____?**

1. **pat** (/p/ /ă/ /t/) _____
2. **leg** (/l/ /ĕ/ /g/) _____
3. **sip** (/s/ /ĭ/ /p/) _____
4. **tub** (/t/ /ŭ/ /b/) _____

5. **rock** (/r/ /ŏ/ /k/) _____
6. **mean** (/m/ /ē/ /n/) _____
7. **joke** (/j/ /ō/ /k/) _____
8. **fast** (/f/ /ă/ /s/ /t/) _____

▶ Recording On Recording Form 2, page 28, indicate correct responses with ✓. If a child gives an incorrect word, write that word. If a child gives a sound, write the letter that sound represents between two slash marks, for example, /r/. Write **0** if a child does not respond.

▶ Discontinue Discontinue testing if a child misses three consecutive items after the Practice Items.

## Familiarity with Print

*Master 1*

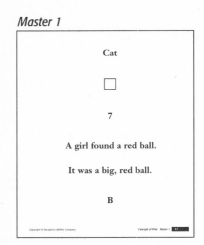

### CONCEPTS OF PRINT

▶ Direction Now I'm going to ask you to find some things on this page. (Show Master 1–Concepts of Print, page 21 .)

▶ Practice Items **Show me which of these is a number.** (Show correct response, if necessary.) **Which of these is a square? Point to the square.** (Show correct response, if necessary.)

▶ Assessment Items (Provide no additional help with these items.)

**1. Show me which of these is a letter standing all by itself—just one letter by itself.**

**2. Show me which of these is a word standing all by itself—just one word by itself.**

**3. Show me which of these are sentences.**

**4. If I were reading these sentences, show me where I would start reading them.** (With your finger draw an oval around the two sentences.)

| | |
|---|---|
| wonderful | won |
| in | introduction |
| tell | television |
| Chrysanthemums | Chris |

**5–6. Point your finger to show which way I would go if I were reading these sentences.** (If a child stops at the end of the sentence, ask the following question.) **Where would I go next? Show me.** (5—left to right) (6—return sweep)

**7. This sentence** (point to first sentence) **says, *A girl found a red ball.*** (Point to the sentence.) **I'm going to read the words again slowly. I want you to touch each of the words in the sentence with your finger as I say the words.** (Have the child point to the first word. Then say, **"Move your finger to show the word I'm reading."**) (Read each word slowly as you continue reading the sentence.)

**8.** (Show Master 2–Spoken/Written Word Correspondence, page 22. Point to the first pair of words.) **Look at these two words. One of them is the word *won* and the other is the word *wonderful*. Which of these words is *won*?** Use the same directions for ***in, introduction; tell, television;*** and ***Chris, chrysanthemums.***

▶ **Recording** On Recording Form 2, page 28, indicate correct responses with ✓. Write **0** if the child does not respond.

▶ **Discontinue** If a child misses four of the first six items, items 7 and 8 can be omitted and assumed to be incorrect.

*Master 3*

| | | | |
|---|---|---|---|
| C | H | B | K |
| E | O | R | V |
| J | A | M | U |
| X | P | S | Y |
| T | D | Q | F |
| N | W | G | Z |
| L | I | | |

## LETTER NAMING

▶ **Directions** (Show Master 3–Letter Naming, Capital Letters, page 23. Do not provide any help with these items or tell the child if answers are wrong or right.)

▶ **Assessment Items**

**1. I'd like you to tell me the names of these letters. What letter is this?**

*Note: You may point to the letter or use index cards or an index card with a "window" cut in it to show one letter at a time. Move left to right across the rows of letters.*

**2.** (Show Master 4–Letter Naming, Lower Case Letters, page 24.) **Now, I'd like you to tell me the names of these letters. What letter is this?**

▶ **Recording** On Recording Form 3, page 29, indicate correct responses with ✓. If a child gives an incorrect letter, record the letter the child gave. Write **0** if the child does not respond.

▶ **Discontinue** Discontinue testing if a child is unable to identify any of the first ten capital letters.

*Master 4*

| | | | |
|---|---|---|---|
| e | a | o | c |
| h | n | u | b |
| g | v | i | z |
| p | r | j | x |
| d | y | w | l |
| s | k | t | q |
| f | m | | |

# Beginning Reading and Writing

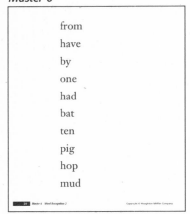

**Master 5**

| | |
|---|---|
| the | that |
| of | is |
| and | he |
| to | are |
| in | as |
| you | with |
| for | his |
| it | they |
| was | at |
| on | this |

**Master 6**

| |
|---|
| from |
| have |
| by |
| one |
| had |
| bat |
| ten |
| pig |
| hop |
| mud |

## WORD RECOGNITION

▶ **Directions** (Show Master 5–Word Recognition 1, page 25. Do not provide any help with these items or tell the child if answers are wrong or right.)

▶ **Assessment Items**

**1. Try to read these words for me.  What is this word?**

*Note: Move down the columns of words. If a child cannot read most of the words, you may wish to ask for the sound the word begins with.  Do this only for words beginning with consonants.*

**2.** (Show Master 6–Word Recognition 2, page 26.) **Now, try to read these words. What is this word?**

▶ **Recording** On Recording Form 3, page 29, indicate correct responses with ✓. If a child gives an incorrect word, record the word given.  If nonsense words or individual sounds are given, represent what the child said phonetically. Write **0** if a child does not respond.

▶ **Discontinue** Discontinue after five consecutive incorrect responses, failure to respond, or a combination of both.

*Note 1: The last five words on the Word Recognition 2 list are not high-frequency words, but are phonetically regular words.  If a child identifies at least five high-frequency words at the top of the list on Word Recognition 1, you should check to see if he/she can identify any of the last five phonetically regular words.*

*Note 2: This is not a timed task; however, if after approximately ten seconds, a child makes no response, say, "Please make a try.  What do you think this word might be?"  If there is still no response, move to the next item.*

## WORD WRITING

▶ **Directions** (Give the child a sheet of unlined paper.  Use one side of the paper for Word Writing.)

▶ **Assessment Items Do you know how to write any words?  Write as many words as you can.** (If necessary, use the following questions as prompts.)  **Can you write your name?  Names of people in your family? Can you write the names of any animals?  Any colors?  Are there any other words you can write?**

*Note: These are the only prompts that should be used.  Use as many of the suggested prompts as necessary if a child stops writing and has not reached the time limit.*

► **Time Limits** It is suggested that you set a time limit of three minutes for kindergarten children and five minutes for first grade children.

► **Recording** The child will be recording the responses; however, it is very important that when a child makes very incomplete or variable responses, that you note, next to what the child has written, what he/she was trying to write. Make note of any proper names that are unusual.

Do not allow a child to copy words from any source. If it appears that copying took place, ask the child to read the words. If he/she cannot read the words, do not give credit for them.

## SENTENCE DICTATION

► **Directions** (For Sentence Dictation, use the unmarked side of the unlined paper that was used for Word Writing.)

► **Assessment Items** **I want you to try to write a sentence for me. I will tell you the sentence and then repeat it one word at a time. If you are not sure about how to write a word, write any letters that you know for the sounds you hear in the word. Try to write this sentence.** (Say the complete sentence and then say each of the words of the sentence slowly but do not artificially stretch out the pronunciation of individual words.)

### 1. The cat is on Jill's bed.

*Note: If needed, the following prompt may be used up to two times per sentence. "Think about the sounds in the word _____. Write the letters for any sounds you hear in _____."*

### 2. Pam can't find her sock.

*Note: Use the second sentence for all children unless a child fails to write any correct letters for sentence one.*

### 3. My sister and her best friend went to lunch today.

*Note: Use the third sentence only for children who can represent most of the sounds in sentences one and two.*

► **Recording** The child will, in effect, record the responses; however, it is very important, when a child makes very incomplete or variable responses, that you note what the child is trying to write.

# Scoring and Interpreting the Results of the Emergent Literacy Survey

## Phonemic Awareness

### RHYME

▶ **Scoring** The scoring of this subtest is clear and objective. One point is awarded for every correct response.

Score responses as correct if they rhyme, even if they are nonsense words. For example, if a child gave the response *jat* as a rhyming word for *bat,* it would be scored as correct.

▶ **Interpretation** Rhyme is considered by many to be the most fundamental of the phonemic awareness skills. Expect a perfect or near perfect (7 of 8 items) performance on this test as an indication of a child's knowledge of and ability to use rhyme.

### BEGINNING SOUNDS

▶ **Scoring** One point is awarded for each correct response. Expect children to respond correctly to all or nearly all (7 of 8) items on this test as an indication they have ability to recognize beginning sounds.

▶ **Interpretation** The concept of beginning sound is an important one for learning to read. Some researchers suggest that this is a more advanced skill than that of familiarity with rhyme; however, many end-of-kindergarten children perform slightly better on a measure of ability to recognize beginning sounds than on a rhyme recognition task. These results may reflect the fact that some kindergarten teachers concentrate more instruction on the concept of beginning sound than on that of rhyme.

### BLENDING ONSETS AND RIMES

▶ **Scoring** One point is awarded for each correct response. There is only one correct answer for each of these items.

▶ **Interpretation** On the surface this looks like an extremely easy task; in reality, it is a very difficult one for young children.

The ability to blend onsets and rimes is a more advanced phonemic awareness skill than that of rhyme or beginning sounds. Performance on this task is highly predictive of a child's success in beginning to learn to read and write. While it may be possible to develop the skill of blending onsets and rimes as a foundation for learning to read, the skill also seems to develop concurrently as children begin to learn to read. When children receive reading instruction, including instruction in blending sounds and in substituting initial consonants with common rimes (phonograms), the skill of blending onsets and rimes also appears to develop. Thus, it would not seem wise to delay reading instruction while trying to develop the skill of blending onsets and rimes. It might be useful, however, to work with onsets and rimes at the auditory level in kindergarten.

## SEGMENTING ONSETS AND RIMES

▶ **Scoring** One point is awarded for each correct response. There is only one correct answer for each of these items.

▶ **Interpretation** This is a very challenging task for young children. The interpretation applied to Blending Onsets and Rimes applies to segmenting as well.

## PHONEME BLENDING

▶ **Scoring** One point is awarded for each correct response. There is only one correct response which represents the correct blending of these phonemes. For example, if a child says *man* instead of *men* for Item 2, it is not credited. However, by writing down a child's incorrect response, you can gather important clues about a child's ability to do the task.

▶ **Interpretation** Manipulating phonemes is among the most challenging phonemic awareness skills – even more challenging than blending onsets and rimes – since the units (phonemes) are quite abstract. In a study conducted early in the school year (October) with first grade children that were identified by their teacher as in the lowest 40% to 60% of the class in terms of emergent reading ability, it was found that on average, these children responded correctly to three of six phonemic blending items very similar to the items in this task. This task is highly predictive of success in learning to read, but delaying reading instruction until a child can manipulate phonemes would not seem appropriate.

## PHONEME SEGMENTATION

▶ **Scoring** Score one point for each correct response. There is only one correct response for each item and all three or four phonemes must be given by the child. You will obtain important clues about a child's ability by writing down incorrect responses.

▶ **Interpretation** This task is even more challenging than the Phoneme Blending task. In the same study cited above, first grade children in the lowest 40% to 60% of the class were successful with two and one-half of six Phoneme Segmentation items. Children who score five or lower across twelve items are at risk of having difficulty learning to read in first grade, and those who score two or lower across twelve items are at considerable risk.

# Familiarity with Print

## CONCEPTS OF PRINT

▶ **Scoring** Score one point for each of the eight items. To score the "tracking" of print Item 7 as correct, there should be clear evidence from the behavior of the child that he/she understands that each spoken word is represented by a printed word. The item should be scored as correct if the child points correctly, but somehow skips or falls behind in one of the words.

Item 8 (Spoken/Written Word Correspondence) has four examples in order to reduce the effects of guessing a correct response. If a child gets at least three of the four items correct, give credit for knowing that a longer spoken word (one with more syllables) is represented by a longer printed word.

▶ **Interpretation** It seems important that children understand fundamental concepts such as what is meant by a word, a letter, and a sentence. These concepts seem to be fairly easy skills for most end-of-kindergarten children.

Children at the beginning stages of learning to read have considerable difficulty in developing the concept that there must be one and only one printed word for each spoken word. Children who memorize text but who cannot yet "track" print sometimes point to a different word for each spoken syllable in a word. Others simply become confused as they point to text and repeat sentences they memorize. They sometimes say all the words before coming to the end of a sentence, or they run out of printed words before they finish saying a sentence. Children who are just beginning to develop the concept that there must be one printed word for each spoken word often indicate confusion when they end up with too many or not enough printed words for spoken words.

Item 8 is a fairly unusual item in a Concepts of Print task, but it is one that is predictive of success in learning to read. The task is designed to determine whether or not a child has developed the concept that spoken words which have a greater number of syllables would need to be represented by longer printed words than short, one-syllable words. While we wouldn't expect young children to be able to explain this concept, children who have more experiences with print appear to develop an understanding of it.

## LETTER NAMING

▶ **Scoring** One point is awarded for each correctly identified letter name.

▶ **Interpretation** A child's ability to learn letter names has long been associated with success in beginning reading. Knowing letter names is necessary in order to follow classroom directions, and many letter names are a clue to learning letter sounds. Most end-of-kindergarten children are able to name most letter names.

## Beginning Reading and Writing

## WORD RECOGNITION

▶ **Scoring** One point is awarded for each word that is correctly identified.

▶ **Interpretation** On average, end-of-kindergarten children will recognize only about three of the first fifteen words on the Word Recognition 1 Master. The first ten words on the list are among the most frequently used words in the English language; the last five words on the Word Recognition 2 Master represent phonetically regular words following consonant-vowel-consonant patterns and containing short vowel sounds. Fifteen additional high-frequency words are included on the list (items 11–25). Thus, the list offers an opportunity to assess both high-frequency vocabulary and phonetically regular vocabulary.

## WORD WRITING

▶ **Scoring** As noted in the Directions for giving this test, it is very important that the examiner make notes of what a child is writing if the writing is not clear and the child is definitely trying to write words. Words must be correctly spelled to be credited on this subtest. A child's ability to phonetically represent a word is measured on the Sentence Dictation task. Some words are very easy and clear to score. Proper names can be more difficult, and if there is any doubt the examiner should ask the child to read the words. When in doubt, credit the child with the word. Do not penalize the child for poorly shaped letters or letters that are reversed, such as *b, d,* and *p.*

▶ **Interpretation** This is a measure of a child's beginning writing fluency. On average, end-of-kindergarten children can write four words. They are most likely to be able to write their own name, sometimes their last name, generic family names like *mom,* and the names of other members of their family.

## SENTENCE DICTATION

▶ **Scoring** A child may score up to 67 points on this measure. Some phonemic boundaries are difficult to determine and somewhat arbitrary, therefore, for sake of reliability and consistency, the number of phonemes in the sentences are as follows:

/Th/e/ /c/a/t/ /i/s/ /o/n/ /J/i/ll/'s/ /b/e/d/. (Total=16)

/P/a/m/ /c/a/n/'t/ /f/i/n/d/ /h/er/ /s/o/ck/. (Total=16)

/M/y/ /s/i/s/t/er/ /a/n/d/ /h/er/ /b/e/s/t/ /f/r/ie/n/d/ /w/e/n/t/ /t/o/ /l/u/n/ch/ /t/o/d/ay/. (Total=35)

A child receives one point for each phoneme that is represented. It is often necessary for the examiner to make some notes on the page to indicate which phonemes from the dictated words are being represented. It would be impossible to score the productions of children who are just beginning to write without such notes.

Credit as correct any letter that could represent the sounds heard in these words, for example, *k* for *c* in *cat; z* for *s* in *is*; or *u* for *a* in *was*, *G* for *J* in *Jill's*. Credit a child for representing the *er* in *her* or *sister* if the child writes *er* or just *r*.

▶ **Interpretation** This is an excellent way of measuring children's growing awareness of sounds, ability to write letters, and ability to associate letters and sounds. An average score for end-of-kindergarten children on the first two sentences has been found to be 8 out of the 32 points. Some first grade children may achieve perfect or near-perfect scores on the first two sentences.

# Cat

□

7

**A girl found a red ball.**

**It was a big, red ball.**

**B**

wonderful                    won

in                    introduction

tell                    television

Chrysanthemums                    Chris

C     H     B     K

E     O     R     V

J     A     M     U

X     P     S     Y

T     D     Q     F

N     W     G     Z

L     I

| | | | |
|---|---|---|---|
| e | a | o | c |
| h | n | u | b |
| g | v | i | z |
| p | r | j | x |
| d | y | w | l |
| s | k | t | q |
| f | m | | |

the

of

and

to

in

you

for

it

was

on

that

is

he

are

as

with

his

they

at

this

from

have

by

one

had

bat

ten

pig

hop

mud

**Child's Name** _____ **27**

**Examiner** _____ **Date** _____

## Rhyme

1. bat _____

2. head _____

3. fan _____

4. got _____

5. rug _____

6. be _____

7. fog _____

8. mill _____

## Beginning Sounds

1. /s/ ink _____

2. /p/ ie _____

3. /m/ ore _____

4. /d/ onkey _____

5. /l/ ion _____

6. /f/ ast _____

7. /ch/ ildren _____

8. /b/ alloon _____

## Blending Onsets and Rimes __

1. /m/ an — man _____

2. /f/ all — fall _____

3. /t/ able — table _____

4. /b/ ill — bill _____

5. /r/ at — rat _____

6. /g/ old — gold _____

7. /m/ other — mother _____

8. /l/ earn — learn _____

## Segmenting Onsets and Rimes

1. /f/ fit (it) _____

2. /g/ gate (ate) _____

3. /s/ sink (ink) _____

4. /l/ land (and) _____

5. /b/ bend (end) _____

6. /p/ pup (up) _____

7. sh/ shape (ape) _____

8. k/ couch (ouch) _____

**Child's Name** _____

**Examiner** _____ **Date** _____

## Phoneme Blending

1. /t/ /ă/ /p/ (tap) _____

2. /m/ /ĕ/ /n/ (men) _____

3. /j/ /ŏ/ /g/ (jog) _____

4. /k/ /ŭ/ /t/ (cut) _____

5. /l/ /ĭ/ /d/ (lid) _____

6. /b/ /ī/ /k/ (bike) _____

7. /w/ /ā/ /v/ (wave) _____

8. /s/ /ŏ/ /f/ /t/ (soft) _____

## Phoneme Segmentation

1. pat /p/ /ă/ /t/ _____

2. leg /l/ /ĕ/ /g/ _____

3. sip /s/ /ĭ/ /p/ _____

4. tub /t/ /ŭ/ /b/ _____

5. rock /r/ /ŏ/ /k/ _____

6. mean /m/ /ē/ /n/ _____

7. joke /j/ /ō/ /k/ _____

8. fast /f/ /ă/ /s/ /t/ _____

## Concepts of Print

1. letter _____

2. word _____

3. sentences _____

4. where start reading _____

5. left to right _____

6. return sweep _____

7. voice/print match _____

8. written/spoken word correspondence _____

**Child's Name** _____

**Examiner** _____  **Date** _____

## Letter Name Identification

| | | | |
|---|---|---|---|
| C _____ | e _____ | | |
| H _____ | a _____ | | |
| B _____ | o _____ | | |
| K _____ | c _____ | | |
| E _____ | h _____ | | |
| O _____ | n _____ | | |
| R _____ | u _____ | | |
| V _____ | b _____ | | |
| J _____ | g _____ | | |
| A _____ | v _____ | | |
| M _____ | i _____ | | |
| U _____ | z _____ | | |
| X _____ | p _____ | | |
| P _____ | r _____ | | |
| S _____ | j _____ | | |
| Y _____ | x _____ | | |
| T _____ | d _____ | | |
| D _____ | y _____ | | |
| Q _____ | w _____ | | |
| F _____ | l _____ | | |
| N _____ | s _____ | | |
| W _____ | k _____ | | |
| G _____ | t _____ | | |
| Z _____ | q _____ | | |
| L _____ | f _____ | | |
| I _____ | m _____ | | |

## Word Recognition

| | | | |
|---|---|---|---|
| 1. the _____ | 27. ten _____ |
| 2. of _____ | 28. pig _____ |
| 3. and _____ | 29. hop _____ |
| 4. to _____ | 30. mud _____ |
| 5. in _____ | |
| 6. you _____ | |
| 7. for _____ | |
| 8. it _____ | |
| 9. was _____ | |
| 10. on _____ | |
| 11. that _____ | |
| 12. is _____ | |
| 13. he _____ | |
| 14. are _____ | |
| 15. as _____ | |
| 16. with _____ | |
| 17. his _____ | |
| 18. they _____ | |
| 19. at _____ | |
| 20. this _____ | |
| 21. from _____ | |
| 22. have _____ | |
| 23. by _____ | |
| 24. one _____ | |
| 25. had _____ | |
| 26. bat _____ | |

# Emergent Literacy Survey
## Summary Form

Child's Name _____  Child's Date of Birth _____

Examiner _____

| Phonemic Awareness | Area Assessed | Assessment 1 Date _____ | Assessment 2 Date _____ | Assessment 3 Date _____ |
|---|---|---|---|---|
| | Rhyme | _____/8 | _____/8 | _____/8 |
| | Beginning Sounds | _____/8 | _____/8 | _____/8 |
| | Blending Onsets and Rimes | _____/8 | _____/8 | _____/8 |
| | Segmenting Onsets and Rimes | _____/8 | _____/8 | _____/8 |
| | Phoneme Blending | _____/8 | _____/8 | _____/8 |
| | Phoneme Segmentation | _____/8 | _____/8 | _____/8 |
| **Familiarity with Print** | Concepts of Print | _____/8 | _____/8 | _____/8 |
| | Letter Naming | _____/52 | _____/52 | _____/52 |
| **Beginning Reading & Writing** | Word Recognition | _____/30 | _____/30 | _____/30 |
| | Word Writing | _____(words) | _____(words) | _____(words) |
| | Sentence Dictation | _____/67 | _____/67 | _____/67 |
| | Comments | | | |

**INVITATIONS**
TO LITERACY

ISBN 0-395-80612-7

90000>

9 780395 806128

Houghton Mifflin

Boston   Atlanta   Dallas   Geneva, Illinois   Palo Alto   Princeton

1-34798-**K-2**